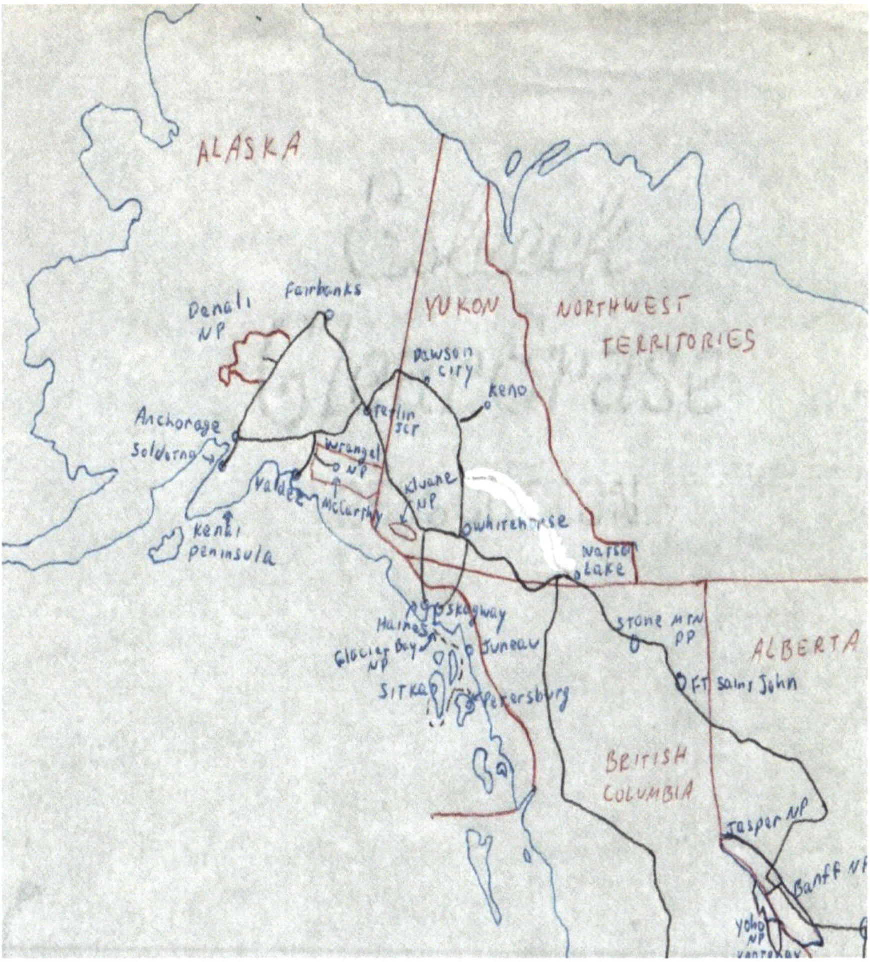

ALASKA
YUKON
NORTHWEST TERRITORIES
Denali NP
Fairbanks
Dawson City
Keno
Anchorage
Soldotna
Tetlin JCT
Wrangell NP
Valdez
McCarthy
Kluane NP
Whitehorse
Watson Lake
Kenai Peninsula
Skagway
Haines
Stone Mtn PP
ALBERTA
Glacier Bay NP
Juneau
FT Saint John
SITKA
Petersburg
BRITISH COLUMBIA
Jasper NP
Banff NP
Yoho NP
Kootenay

Wild eyes of life
camouflaged in the dark,
Watching us hike in Kluane
National Park

Totem poles in
Kitwancool,
Indian legend carved in
wood with tool

The fluffiest clouds I've seen

The dark ones sprinkle their
drops

To paint the forest green

Trees remind me of green tipped Crayolas
East Glacier Loop Trail, Juneau Mendenhall Glacier

Chilkoot Lake

Eagles soar,
rehabilitate in their
mews

Silence, nature –
nurtures my inner
muse
Chilkoot Lake

S.S. Klondike, Whitehorse

Bull kelp, cow parsnip and bladderwrack

Nature's food we tasted aboard a sea kayak

Glacier Bay National Park, Gustavus

Suddenly our path
looks like it ended
Indian River Trail, Sitka

Steps later - the stairs
beckon us to find

The waterfall is splendid

Ice crystals give
off a blue glow

At the Mendenhall
Glacier in Juneau

Arrived in
Petersburg at 11 pm

Settled at Sandy Beach
in the
land of the Midnight Sun

Roller Coaster waves on the
Nenana River

Despite our waterproof suit, we
had to shiver

Denali Raft Adventures

In Denali, found a home,
Over a hill in
Polychrome

Blazed our own trail in
the backcountry

Ate on a hill near a
caribou lunchery

Two red fox – over the hill
they didn't know

Brown bear sleeping
in the snow
Denali National Park

Roadside – unlikely spot
for Dall sheep to roam
An awesome sight
before going home

www.ingramcontent.com/pod-product-compliance
Lightning Source LLC
Chambersburg PA
CBHW040255240726
48664CB00001B/403